It's Time for You

Getting unstuck means facing pain... emotional, spiritual, social or financial. You may have to face things that you have buried deep within your soul.

Getting unstuck means having to shift your energy. You will have to let go of something in order to grab hold of the cognitive tools you need to get to your next level of success.

Getting unstuck means giving yourself a jump-start to reach beyond your limits and achieve success. It will free you to live the life that you were designed to live.

Clestine, The Purpose Coach

Knuggets of Knowledge to Get Unstuck
Copyright © 2007 by Clestine I. Herbert

Cover design by SMPR, Inc.
Edited by Allison Rushton
Published by BookSurge Publishing

Available through Amazon.com, Abebooks.com, Alibris.com, Borders.com, Target.com and DivineDiscipline.com

Author Email: Clestine@DivineDiscipline.com

For permission, write to:
Clestine I. Herbert
Divine Discipline
P.O. Box 4019
Spring Hill, FL 34611,
or *Info@DivineDiscipline.com.*

To book the author to speak at your event, business meeting or church, contact us at Info@DivineDiscipline.com, 813-343-4112 or http://www.divinediscipline.com/speaker-request.php

ISBN-10: 1-4196-6951-6
ISBN-13: 978-1-4196-6951-4

Printed in the United States of America.

Knuggets *of* Knowledge
To Get Unstuck

Practical wisdom to help you get unstuck and
achieve success in any area of life.

Clestine I. Herbert

What People Are Saying about This Book:

"My friend Clestine speaks with a pure and authentic voice, sharing the wisdom of the ages as she has come to know it. She is a dedicated coach and a model of excellence for others!"

Millicent St. Claire
Accelerated Learning Expert
Atlanta, Georgia

"As I read those golden nuggets penned by Clestine, I felt as if I was the director of a thrilling, suspenseful, adventure movie, and the leading star was me!"

Celeste Cirigliano
Spring Hill, Florida

"*Knuggets of Knowledge* is a great peak performance enhancer for anyone who wants to reach beyond their limits. Clestine Herbert propels you to higher performance on every level with useful *Knuggets of Knowledge* and empowering affirmations to support each *knugget*. And the 'Getting Unstuck' questions in each chapter make it easy to apply the information to your individual and present circumstances."

Tara Coyt
The Write Author Coach
Coyt Communications
Atlanta, Georgia

"Clestine Herbert's *Knuggets of Knowledge* is a wonderful book that could change your destiny. It helps you focus on your goals and life plan to lead a successful and fulfilling life."

Pasha Baker
President & CEO
Posh Business Solutions and Posh Diversity & Human Resources
Tampa, Florida

This Book Is Dedicated to...

My parents and siblings: You have been there for me in the good and the bad times. You never let me go. You continued to encourage me, love me, support me and pray for me. *I dedicate this book to you* and hope that this book will help you to dig deep in areas where you have been afraid to scratch the surface. I pray that you get unstuck so that you can live the liberated life that God created for you. I love you all forever and know that God will bless you forever.

My nieces and nephews: Je-Wan, Ajenaé and JeShaun... *I love you sooooo much and am proud of what you have accomplished in life thus far*. You are very special to me and I know God has a special purpose for each of you. Shenaje, Alesia, Rian and DJ... *I have grafted you into my hearts as my nieces and nephews*.

I don't want any of you to let anyone tell you that you won't be successful. God has created each of us with *amazing* abilities to achieve success. The ones that are successful are the ones that realize this little secret. Discover who God created you to be, then *do all that you can* to make sure that you achieve it. *I dedicate this book to you*, praying that you will not allow anyone (except God) or anything to get you stuck in life. You are destined to grow up to be men and women of greatness. I see it. I've spoken it. Now achieve it.

Acknowledgements to...

My Heavenly Father... Abba: Why you chose me to empower others through speaking, coaching and writing I'll never know, but I love it! I praise you for being you and for always being there for me. Thank you for never giving up on me. Thank you for the wisdom you poured into me. Thank you for being patient with me and never letting me go. Your timing is always perfect. Thank you for allowing me to take this journey. It is more exciting with you. This is just the beginning of an amazing journey, and I can't wait to see what more amazing and awesome things you have in store for me. I love you Lord!

My Parents... Melvin and Edna: Thank you for your continued support during this process. Though it took longer than you would have liked [☺], you still encouraged me financially, with *unspoken* words, prayers and a heartfelt desire to see me achieve success. I know God is going to bless you abundantly for all that you have done for me. Watch and see! I love you forever.

My siblings... Eudine and Jessel: You have always believed in me no matter what. When I left corporate America to start my journey as an empowerment speaker and life coach, you did not discourage me. You believed in me and encouraged me to be who God created me to be. You love and encourage me even when you don't understand. You have always been in my corner and for that I am forever grateful. You both have some awesome, powerful gifts, and I can't wait until the world sees them. I love you both deeply.

Mary and Reynold Caleb, Thelma and Owen Guthrie: You 'adopted' me as one of your daughters. Treated me as one of your own children. You always supported me, believed in me and fed me (yum, yum!). During the tough times you encouraged me and you were there for me even when you didn't know it. I love you and will be forever grateful

Virginia and Lou: Thank you for your prayers, encouragement and support. Your prayers for me, along with others, are what helped me through. Everyone in life needs a life coach for accountability, but I know that each person also needs an intercessor to help propel them through challenges. *(Please start praying me through the next book ☺). I love you both.* Thank you forever.

Tallie, Del, Jeremy and Rick: Thank you for being forever friends with the right amount of *testosterone* to push me through. You didn't just tell me what I wanted to hear but also what I needed to hear. You coached me, encouraged me and (when you felt I needed it) assertively pressed me through each stage of my journey to get unstuck and reach beyond my *perceived* limits so I could finish this book and start another chapter in my life. You all are special to me.

Donna, Kena, Olga, Jasmine, Merle, Nicole and Ilyn: At different points of this journey, God used you to encourage me. Oftentimes, I don't think you knew it. You encouraged me with your own struggles and achievements. You each supported me in your own unique way and that was appreciated. You are all powerful, successful women of God, and I love each of you. I am thankful that He brought you into my life.

Message from an Unstuck Author

I realized toward the end of this book that I too had to get unstuck. Imagine that! An author writing a book to help people get unstuck who had to get unstuck from the challenges of writing and publishing this book.

In this book you are receiving nuggets of wisdom I obtained from experiences I've had in the last few years of my life. I will honestly tell you that while writing this book, I got stuck in the middle. The cheerleaders had gone home, but the pressure was still on. My excitement had faded, and I just wanted the project to be finished. Sound familiar? I kept going (after a long break) because I knew that this book wasn't just for me, but for the *thousands* of people that it would empower to get unstuck, get going and reach beyond their perceived limits to get to their next level of success.

Please make sure you complete the exercises in the **Getting Unstuck** section at the end of each chapter. You will begin to see areas in your life that you need to move forward in or re-evaluate. Whatever the case may be, take it from me, all the pain and discomfort that you may feel from getting unstuck is well worth it. It is liberating. Let's not procrastinate anymore. Start reading this book and get unstuck.

Clestine I. Herbert

Clestine, The Purpose Coach &
Empowerment Speaker

Table of Contents

Introduction

Reach

beyond your limits

A ffirm yourself with me, *"My next level of success is waiting for me, and I am going to reach it!"* If you pause after making that statement, for just a moment you might possibly hear your *perceived* limits whispering, or even yelling. They often begin their sentences like this:

"I can't..."

"I wish I could..."

"I'm not sure if I can...."

"I don't have time to..."

Whether you are an executive in a large corporation, an owner of a small business, employed or a homemaker, we all have perceived limits. Some we are aware of and some we are not. But for most, we have embraced these limits as truth. We have developed beliefs based on limits that were developed from our childhood, our experiences in life or one traumatic experience. We now live by these limits and allow them to define our lives, to develop our pace. It's time to let your inner voice of success guide you to the next level.

Mental limits (limitations of our mind) are some of the most damaging, inhibiting limits we will ever encounter. Somewhere along the line, we may have been told we cannot, so we don't. We don't question it. We don't even try it. Limits, unfortunately, are the dividing line (or should I say dividing *lie*) between the success life has to offer, and life as it is now.

Question: Are you ready to go to *your* next level? Some of you are saying "yes." My next question to you is: *"Are you sure?"* I meet countless people who talk about what they want to do. The great things they desire to accomplish. What it will look like once they get there. How it will benefit others. But when asked what they are doing to reach those goals, their perceived limits answer. It is a limiting voice that chokes the energy out of a person and strips away the ability to break through and *reach beyond your limits*.

People always have a *reason* why they cannot! However, the "why" that should drive us is *why* you are pursuing this dream. The *why* of your destiny should be strong enough to quiet the voice of your perceived limits.

I have developed a new definition for success. ***Success is a place that is just on the other side of your limits.*** It is that close. If you could see how close you are to *reaching beyond your limits* to attain success, you would be surprised.

This book, ***Knuggets of Knowledge to Get Unstuck,*** is an introduction to my **Reach Beyond Your Limits**™ program. It is filled with little nuggets of wisdom to help you stretch your mind and spirit and reach beyond the *perceived* limits that you have embraced or allowed to be placed on yourself. Some of the nuggets are bite-sized; others are mega nuggets. Either way, this book will help you get unstuck. Maybe you were on your way to success but somehow got sidetracked. Or maybe you need help being pointed in the right direction. Whatever your situation, I hope you won't read this book just one time, but several. Buy one for a friend. Read it at a book club. Utilize it to reformat your thinking and get yourself unstuck, so that you can *reach beyond your limits* to the next level of success.

Instead of allowing your limits to define how you live your life, *or* an area of your life, let this moment be the deciding moment to *reach beyond your limits*. If you don't remember anything else, remember this: *your success is waiting for you.* Stop listening to the voice of limitations and start listening to the voice of your success. Of course it takes time and effort, but you can empower yourself to reach beyond. ***Reach Beyond Your Limits***™ is a new program that will empower you to stop, think and *reach beyond your limits*! There are three main principals that one must use to reach beyond his or her limits:

1. Think beyond
2. Plan beyond
3. Perform beyond.

I would like to encourage you to inquire about the **Reach Beyond Your Limits**™ program. This program will not only help you to get unstuck, it will also reprogram your thought process and habits so that you can stay unstuck.

In addition to providing this little book as an appetizer to **Reach Beyond Your Limits**™, I have designed coaching programs, seminars, keynotes and CDs to help you do what it takes to reach your next level. *You can do it!* We each need someone or something to give us a nudge and get us unstuck. Executives, you need to get to your next level. Small business owners, it's time to get to your next level. Homemakers, embrace this and get to your next level. Whatever your profession, it's time to get unstuck and get to your next level in life.

Have you been procrastinating or living in fear? Let *Knuggets of Knowledge to Get Unstuck* wake up your spirit, give you a nudge and get you unstuck. This first book was created to help whet your appetite. It is designed to give you a nudge, or wake up some part of you. My next book in this series will take a more in-depth look at reaching beyond one's *perceived* limits and acquiring success. My prayer is that this book will motivate you to start the process of reaching for success.

Feel free to email me and let me know how you enjoyed this appetizer. Or better yet, invite me to speak at your next event or company meeting to help some of your attendees *get unstuck*. Contact me at Clestine@DivineDiscipline.com. Let this be the beginning of a successful journey that we take together. Enjoy, and empowered reading to you!

From Stuck to Unstuck

*A **True** Story*

She was a young woman who was shy and insecure deep down inside. She was stuck. She had a fleeting sense of her ability to lead others, but she wasn't sure in what. Her vision of who she was, was blinded by her perceptions of her own identity. Yet, when she looked at others, she saw their great talent and wondered why she didn't have special talents of her own. Oh, she knew there were things she was capable of doing, but she felt that she didn't have talents that she did exceptionally well. She felt she didn't shine or stand out in any area of her life. However, that was not true. Her perception of herself had her stuck. She felt mundane. Just average. A part of the crowd lost in a sea of people. She was officially stuck. Stuck by her own mental and emotional barriers. Stuck in her own insecurities.

In Corporate America, she excelled at her craft. She said the right things, wore professional suites and even wore an air of confidence. Yet deep down inside there was someone else that needed to be seen. She felt as if she was going through the motions of life. Why? Because, she was still stuck.

She failed to recognize her own talents for organizing people and events. She failed to acknowledge her ability to lead people. She failed to understand that she had an aura that made people feel comfortable coming to her and bearing their soul. She failed to recognize that her colleagues, friends and even strangers valued her advice and that she was an encourager; always encouraging others to press forward. You see on the outside, what the world saw was a caring, confident, multitalented trustworthy, powerful woman, but inside she felt differently. She didn't recognize that she was a starter and creator; a pioneer who goes beyond the norm and paves the way for others to follow. She didn't recognize what others saw because she was stuck. She was stuck in a prison of wanting to be liked and accepted. Stuck in the area of wanting approval. Stuck in disapproval of herself. Just stuck in her mental and emotional prison.

As she grew, she acquired well paying exciting jobs as an engineer, but she still felt empty inside and not quite capable.

Where was she supposed to be? Who was she supposed to be? What was she really supposed to be doing? Who was she created to be? These questions often haunted her soul.

As time marched on, she began to recognize that she really did have exceptional talents and skills. She began to recognize her value and that she was a valuable woman. However, she was climbing that Corporate ladder and as she continued to be promoted her salary increased. Ah yes, the almighty dollar. How could she possibly let go of that. However, she finally began to realize that engineering was not what she was created to do. But the money was so good! Again she was stuck! This time she was imprisoned by the desire for the almighty dollar. She was following the dollar signs instead of following her heart. Boy was she stuck!

After years of searching, reflecting, praying, persevering and achieving, she became free. Free of the mental barriers that had her imprisoned for years. Free to pursue the success that was waiting for her and was rightfully hers. Free of an unhealthy desire for the almighty dollar. Free to be truly successful. Free to be who she was created to be. Aaah! She was finally *unstuck*.

Who is this woman? *That woman is me.* A woman that grew up to be a powerful yet practical, energetic yet engaging international speaker, life coach and author.

So What About You?

Some of you have made many accomplishments in life and I want to commend you for that, yet there is an area of your life where you have been stuck. You've been stuck for weeks, months or years. Without knowing your situation, I will venture to say that it is your mental barriers that are keeping you from moving forward. For some it is possibly because you are waiting for that great something or someone to propel you forward. Yet for others, it is a lack of desire or willingness to make the effort or take the time to do what needs to be done. Getting unstuck takes time, *your* energy (effort) and *your* determination, among other things, but those are a good start.

Too many people whether a corporate executive, an engineer, an investor, an administrator, store clerk, a housewife, or an actor are stuck. Stuck in unhappiness. Stuck in a dead-end job. Stuck in their negative thinking. Stuck in unhealthy relationships. It's time to get unstuck in at least one area of your life.

The nuggets of wisdom in this book are a collection of applicable lessons I learned to help me get unstuck from my mental, emotional and spiritual prisons. If you apply over and over again everything from this book that resonates with you, until it becomes a part of you, you will get unstuck. You deserve to live a fulfilling life. You deserve to experience the freedom and power you experience from truly being who you were created to be. You deserve to be unstuck. *Be a part of the Get Unstuck revolution.* Now let's get started.

Knugget #1

Knowledge
is NOT power.

Applied
knowledge is power.

I have met many people who are knowledgeable. They keep up with the latest world news or pop news and can debate almost any subject. They are able to articulate their opinions well and influence those around them. But take a peek behind closed doors, and you will see non-activity. They are knowledgeable people, yet they don't act on the knowledge that they have. It is a dangerous and unfulfilling place to reside.

My computer is full of information that can empower me to solve a problem or complete a project. However, if I never bother to plug the computer into the electrical outlet or communicate to it through the mouse and/or keyboard, the information is useless.

Seek wisdom and you will find peace, happiness and prosperity in life. Are you walking around like an unplugged computer, carrying knowledge without utilizing it? Are you full of knowledge, but lacking the power of application? Do you sit by the wayside of life watching others struggle without lending a hand? Have you watched yet another person persevere until they attain their *own* dreams? Or are you willing to use and share your knowledge with others? Your knowledge has no value until you turn it into action and do whatever it compels you to do. Knowledge plus action is the formula for acquiring success.

Imagine if someone handed you a suitcase with one million dollars and told you that you can do with it as you wish. Excitedly, you take the suitcase to your home, to the house that needs a new roof, new plumbing and new electrical outlets. You tell every one you meet about the suitcase with a million dollars. *(Of course, I wouldn't recommend that!)*

You tell your good friend who always lends you a hand and was recently in an unfortunate accident that totaled his car that you are now in a position to help him. You tell your neighbor who is trying to send her child to college not to worry. The scenarios continue. You tell everyone about the money, and they can all think of worthwhile ways to use it. Yet the suitcase continues to sit in your house *that is falling apart*. Each day you come home to the suitcase with a million dollars in it. You look at it. You get excited about it. However, you don't do anything with the money. You don't put it in the bank. You don't invest it. You don't try to fix your house. You don't try to help your friends. All you do is get excited about the suitcase with a million dollars in it and tell others about it.

This is what many of us do with our knowledge. Knowledge is priceless. We get excited about it. We tell others about the knowledge we have obtained. However, for many of us, the story ends there. We don't do anything to turn our knowledge into power through action. You need to do something with the knowledge you acquire. Apply it to your own life. Help others by sharing it. Empower yourself by allowing your knowledge to fuel your actions.

Beware! It is easy to gain knowledge, even share it with others, without applying the benefits of wisdom in your own life. *In other words, it is easier to tell others what to do than it is to do it yourself.* Don't fall into that trap. What trap? The trap of having knowledge but never applying it. Challenge yourself. Hold yourself accountable for something. Life was not created for us to just float along and receive whatever crumbs come our way. Life was meant to provide challenges that develop our character muscles and good habits.

It's time to take action! No more delays. Get up and start moving toward your dreams using the knowledge you have obtained. *Get unstuck!* Turn your knowledge into power by applying it in your life today.

Affirmation #1

I will take my knowledge and turn it into power by taking calculated risks.

Getting Unstuck

Making It Personal to You

1. What knowledge have you acquired that you have not put into action?_____

   _____

2. How will you use this knowledge *(notice I said how **will** you and not how **can** you)*?_____

   _____

3. Now write down a dream or goal that you have, but not yet achieved. *(It can be in your personal, professional or spiritual life)*._____

   _____

   _____

   _____

   _____

4. Write down some information *(a piece of knowledge)* that you have obtained that you can use to help you achieve your goal._____

   _____

   _____

5. Now write down *how* you can use this piece of knowledge to help achieve your goal._____

   _____

   _____

   _____

6. What three major steps must you take toward achieving your goal?
   a. Milestone #1:_____
   b. Milestone #2: _____
   c. Milestone #3:_____

7. When do you want to accomplish this goal or dream?____
   _____

8. What will you have to sacrifice (or let go of) to achieve this goal? *(This may be hard to think about, but it is necessary to get unstuck!)*_____
   _____

9. What will you use to motivate you to achieve your goal?
   _____

10. What knowledge do you feel you need to acquire?
   _____
   _____

11. How are you going to acquire this knowledge?_____
   _____

12. When are you going to acquire this knowledge?
   _____

Turn your knowledge into power by acting on it!

Knugget #2

Learn to maintain your *knowledge* gain.

Once you have gained knowledge and applied it, you then have to ensure that knowledge is maintained. Acquiring knowledge doesn't guarantee anything. The knowledge must then be utilized through actions that become habits through repetition and perseverance. Applying and re-applying knowledge acquired helps us to build good habits. However, just like anything else, we have to nurture and maintain it. For example, you discover that walking outside for 30 minutes 3 to 4 times a week has reduced your stress and increased your health. You establish a good routine but then sprain an ankle. You decide to refrain from walking for a few months. Now your ankle is healed, but you are now out of your routine of walking. You're back to your *old* habit of not exercising! Perhaps you could have done sit-ups or lifted hand weights to maintain the habit *(knowledge)* of exercising. Acquiring knowledge does not guarantee that you will develop good habits. It must be repeated and maintained. Exercise what you have learned, share it with others, develop it, but don't lose it.

One of the best ways to maintain the knowledge you have acquired is to use it and develop a good habit based on what you've learned. Developing a habit means repeating particular thoughts or actions until it becomes a natural part of your routine.

You can also maintain your knowledge by acquiring more information about the same subject. Read about it, and also see how other people use it. Discover how this knowledge affects your life. Write it down. Review it periodically and discover why this knowledge is important to you. Look at how your life, or an area of your life, was before and after you started applying the information gained. *Get Unstuck!* Maintain your knowledge.

Affirmation #2

*I will maintain the knowledge I have
acquired by using it repeatedly
and sharing it with others.*

Getting Unstuck

Making It Personal to You

1. Think about the knowledge you gained from **Knugget #1.**
   What will you do to maintain this knowledge?

   _____

   _____

   _____

2. What book(s) or magazine(s) will you read to increase this
   knowledge?_____

3. How often will you review information about this new
   knowledge you've found (daily, weekly, monthly, annually)?__

   _____

4. Who will you share this knowledge with? _____

   _____

   _____

5. How will you share this knowledge with them?_____

   _____

6. What else will you do to maintain this knowledge?

   _____

7. How can you transform this knowledge into a good habit?_____

Knugget #3

The **battle** *is in your* **mind.**
Learn *to manage your*
thoughts.

Managing your thoughts is an essential ingredient to maintaining and enhancing your personal, professional and spiritual life. Obtaining knowledge is not enough. How many people do you know that have attended countless seminars, workshops and church services, only to continue to do the same thing week in and week out? Many, I'm sure. Maybe even you. Once you have acquired the knowledge you seek, you must make a decision that you are going to make a change. Once you have made that decision in your heart, the battle is on! You must now take control of your mind and command it to do what you tell it to do. God has given us the power of choice. We need to choose to tell our minds what to do!

Our brains are made up of several storage areas. Each bit of information has been collected from our experiences (good and bad). What we watch, what we smell, taste, touch or hear determines the knowledge we possess. Our brains catalog and store the information it feels is important. What is stored is not necessarily good for us or true. We have to then do inventory and decide what is true, or good, for us. Many of us have never taken inventory or organized our mental storage area. So whatever our minds tell us, we believe or do. For example, you are interested in applying for a job. Your mind, based on your experiences or what you have been told in the past, tells you, *"You'll never get this job!"* You start dwelling on that thought, and before you know it, you decide that you should forfeit submitting your resumé. You have just eliminated yourself from what could have been your new job.

Your Thoughts Determine Your Destiny

It has been said that your thoughts become your attitude; your attitude determines your actions; your actions determine your habits; your habits determine your lifestyle and your lifestyle determines your destiny. Your thoughts can drive you to a fulfilling or unfulfilling destiny. The choice is yours. There are too many people who are growing up but not maturing. Maturity can only be developed through patience and wisdom. If you stay in bed for one year, you will become one year older, but whether or not you have matured during that time will be questionable. Maturity dictates that you glean wisdom out of your experiences and learn from your mistakes. Maturity embraces and evolves with life's changes. Maturity means you don't do what everyone else is doing. You do what is right, regardless of what others think or do. In order to reach beyond your limits and achieve success, you must advance to a new level of maturity as well. Manage your thoughts in order to manage your attitude.

When your mind tells you that you can't achieve the goal your heart desires, tell your mind with determination, motivation and energy, *"I will achieve this goal no matter how long it takes."* Don't let your mind control you. You control your mind. In order to achieve success, you must first learn to manage your thoughts. Take the inside-out approach. If you can manage your thoughts, you can manage your destiny.

Affirmation #3

*I will take control of my thoughts
before my thoughts take control of me.*

Getting Unstuck

Making It Personal to You

1. Write down what negative thoughts you continue to tell yourself and believe._____

    _____

2. Why do you have those negative thoughts?_____

    _____

3. Write down positive thoughts (an affirmation) that you can speak in your mind or aloud to replace those thoughts. _____

    _____

    Now say it every time those negative thoughts come to mind.

4. Is there something in your life right now that is continuing to affect you attitude? If so, write it down.

    _____

    _____

5. Try to remember what you were thinking the last time you got upset. Write it down. _____

    _____

6. Now write down how you could have resolved this issue in a more positive yet honest way._____

    _____

    _____

7. Meditate on what you just wrote. Let it sink into your spirit *(i.e. read it over and over again).*

    Now, the next time your mind starts leading you down the wrong path, tell it that you are going to choose to take the right path, then do it!

What Are You Thinking?

Take a few minutes to write down thoughts that you are having in this moment. Either write down what you are thinking or draw a picture of what you are thinking in the space provided below. I call this *throwing-everything-out-on-the-table*. Get everything out of your head. Now spend some time evaluating your thoughts. Write down why you feel you are thinking these thoughts. Categorize them if you can. Are they healthy thoughts that line up with where you want to go? Are they negative thoughts? Do they lead you away from your destiny? Try to clear your head and empty your thoughts *onto the table* before we go onto the next section.

Knugget #4

Manage your emotions
before they manage *you.*

Y our emotions are a product of your thoughts. The question we should be asking ourselves then is, *"What am I thinking?"* When your colleague gets the job that you were going after, do you congratulate them or compose reasons why he or she should not have received the position? When your fellow church member gets the solo that you were practicing for, do you sing the chorus to the best of your ability or sabotage the song? Whatever your emotional response is, you *can* control it. At first it won't be easy, but then getting unstuck is never easy at first.

The reality is that in some situations it is harder to control our emotions than others, but that doesn't mean we can't do it. It may mean that we have to walk away, count to ten, pray or think of something pleasant, but we can do it. Think of it this way. If the President of the United States of America, Oprah Winfrey or some other influential person walked into the room while you were having a heated argument, more than likely you would find the energy and willpower to control your emotions for that moment. If you can do it in front of an influential audience, you can do it anytime, anywhere and with anyone. It takes time, self-control and practice. It's a conscious choice.

You Have a Choice

Every day of our lives we have to make choices. We have to choose to drag ourselves out of bed when really we want to sleep another hour. You choose to forgo dessert so that you can fit into that striking outfit for a long-awaited date. Whatever path you end up on, the fact remains that we make choices every day. Some are good, and some bad. But wouldn't it behoove us to make the best choices so that we can reap the best results later? Yes!

Countless people claim that another person has made their life miserable. In fact, I am quite sure you can find a room full of people to agree with this statement. However, the truth is that you can learn to control your own happiness. James Blake, a tennis pro, is living proof of this truth. During a professional tennis match in 2004, James dived forward to get a shot only to trip and be propelled head-first into the steel net post. He then turned his head and fell on his neck, snapping it. While lying in his hospital bed, his coach said, "You have two choices; you can either laugh or cry." James chose to laugh. The doctors were skeptical as to whether or not he would be able to play tennis again. But with perseverance and a positive attitude, James was back in the game a few months later.

Each day we encounter crossroads and must make a choice. Oftentimes, we have only a split-second to make a decision, although the consequences of the choice we make can affect us, and those close to us, for the rest of our lives. Using wisdom when responding may be painful or hard up front, but the long-term rewards are more peace, happiness and prosperity.

Affirmation #4

I will own my behavior.

Getting Unstuck

Making It Personal to You

When you are entering a state of elevated emotions, try some of these techniques:

1. Count to 10 slowly.

2. Breathe in deeply for 3 seconds, and then breathe out slowly for 7 seconds. Repeat this exercise a few times.

3. Manage your self-talk. Tell yourself what is honest and true. Your self-talk should encourage your spirit but not falsely pacify your feelings.

4. Pray. You can't do this alone. We all need help.

5. Choose the voice in your head that is telling you the right thing to do. Listen closely, sometimes it's the quietest voice.

6. If you get emotional in certain situations or with certain people, ask yourself *why*.

7. Think of a recent situation in which you became very emotional, a situation where you later realized that you could have responded in a better way. What was the situation, and how could you have responded in a better way? _____

    _____

    _____

    _____

Check Your Emotional Barometer

Let's check in with your emotional barometer. We're going to check when, with whom and why you may get a rise in your emotions. You can record both negative and positive emotional reactions if you like. Record the information in the table below.

A Person or Situation	Your Emotional Reaction	WHY (Reason)

Now take the time to review the information and think about what you can do to improve your emotional reaction in certain situations. *Tip: Focus on the why column.* This will help you to discover the reason behind this behavior. Discovering and acknowledging *why* is a good start in creating a healthy emotional response in that area.

Knugget #5

You *don't* have to do what your *feelings* tell you to do.

Years ago, while I was in college, *(Wow! That's 20 years ago. My, how time flies)* my mother also decided to further her education in nursing. She worked full-time while going to school part-time. Working nights, 11p.m. to 7a.m., she would often have to go straight from work to school, and then somehow manage to stay awake in class. On occasion she would meet with a friend to study for tests.

One Sunday afternoon, I heard her speaking to herself, or should I say encouraging herself. She was tired and really just wanted to curl up and sleep a little longer, but she knew that she had to meet with her study partner to review some of the data that she didn't understand. She reluctantly got up and made the 30-minute drive to meet her study partner. Hours later, she came in the door beaming. *"I am so glad I didn't follow my feelings and stay at home in bed,"* she said. *"Now I understand the information that I had questions about."* When she took the test the next day, she passed with flying colors.

How many times have you allowed your feelings to dictate what you should or shouldn't do, only to wish later that you had compelled yourself to do what needed to be done? Oftentimes, when we follow our feelings, they lead us down a road of laziness, discouragement, or abandonment. Imagine if my mother had followed her feelings and stayed at home. She probably would not have passed the exam.

Start taking inventory of your feelings. You will notice that oftentimes they will not tell you the wise thing to do. They tell you to say *no* when you should say *yes*. They tell you to say *yes* when you should say *no*. They tell you to stay in bed and rest when you need to get up and get ready for work. They tell you to ignore the ones you love when you should sit down and discuss the situation that hurt your feelings. Whatever the case may be, most of the time, our feelings will lead us down the wrong path.

Overcoming Your Feelings

Learning to listen to wisdom instead of your feelings can be a grueling process for some, yet for others it may be a decision made in a moment. Either way, I guarantee you will not be disappointed. Take the time you need to get into the habit of following wisdom instead of your feelings. Even when writing this book, there were so many times when I had to think about you, the reader, the achiever, rather than my tiredness or frustration. *(Aren't you glad I did?!)*

Here are a few techniques you can use to learn how to overcome your feelings and follow wisdom. Since we each fall under different personality types, you should select which is best for you and work to develop positive habits during the next 3 months.

1. **Pray.** Pray for strength and wisdom to do the right thing.

2. **Read about others.** Read autobiographies of famous people or leaders. You will often read about decisions they had to make against their feelings, so they could follow wisdom.

3. **Write a plan.** Whatever you choose to do, make sure you have a plan. It will help you to stay focused and on track.

4. **Just do it!** The fact remains you can complain or cry all you want, but wisdom remains the same. Wisdom is always there, just waiting for us to catch up to it. Just do it! You'll find that the feelings will go away... *eventually.*

5. **Play music.** Music is good for the soul, I hear. Playing positive music can help motivate us to do something we didn't want to do.

6. **Speak affirmations.** Speak positive affirmations that line up with wisdom and your plans.

7. **Journal.** Journaling is a very powerful tool. Write down how you are feeling, why you are feeling this way and what will happen if you continue to feel this way. Now write down how things will work out if you do what is right, good and wise.

Affirmation #5

*I choose wisdom
over my feelings.*

Getting Unstuck

Making It Personal to You

1. Have you experienced something recently that has upset you? If yes, what?_____

   _____

   _____

2. Are you allowing your feelings to guide you instead of allowing wisdom to guide you? _____

   _____

3. Are you having a hard time getting unstuck in a certain area in your life? In other words, are you stuck in your feelings?_____

4. How does this situation make you feel?_____

   _____

5. What wisdom have you received that can help you?

   _____

6. If you are not using this wisdom, why not?_____

   _____

7. Who can help you get unstuck?_____

8. What will happen if you continue to feel this way?

   _____

9. Now write down how things will work out if you do what is right, good and wise._____

   _____

   _____

   _____

"Wisdom is not a product of schooling but of the life-long attempt to acquire it"

Albert Einstein

Knugget #6

You *don't have to* *experience* *everything.*

L ife is too short to experience everything. Besides, who would want to go through everything, especially the negative experiences? Learn from others. We all have different personalities, different backgrounds and have experienced various circumstances in life. I also recognize that what applies to one person may not apply to another person. However, learning from the experiences of others can oftentimes save us a lifetime of heartache, hardship and pain.

Discovering your personality type will be a good way to help you discover what will be a challenge to you, what will frustrate you, the type of people that you will feel most comfortable around, and the type of situations you may tend to get yourself into. When you know your personality type, you have the insight needed to make adjustments that will make life easier. There is a popular personality test called the *Myers Briggs Personality Test*. This test can be found online at many websites, such as, www.myersbriggs.org, or www.knowyourtype.com. There are also some organizations that allow you to take the Myers Briggs test at a nominal fee. There are other personality tests out there as well, many of which are free. Do your research.

Once you have discovered your personality type, you will discover many things about yourself. I might add that taking a personality test is something that you will probably have to do several times. Why? Because we tend to hide who we are. Sigmund Freud said that our personalities are similar to an iceberg. The majority is hidden deep beneath the surface, so deep that we ourselves may not fully know many facets of our true selves. For example, why do you get upset when certain people say certain things to you? Why are you unable to get anywhere on time? Why do you continue to gravitate toward certain volatile relationships? Why are you so goal-oriented? By learning about yourself, you can melt the iceberg, which will help you to discover the types of situations your personality type tends to get into, as well as positive and negative aspects of your character. Once you discover more about yourself, then you can start doing what it takes to work through your situations in a more positive way.

Learning about yourself can help you evade situations that can cause pain, frustration or delays in your life that could have been avoided had wisdom been used. Something else to consider is that just because something works well for one person, it does not mean that it will work well for you. Know yourself, and stop trying to be like the Joneses. Your life will have more peace and happiness that way. In other words, no one can be a better you than you. *Get unstuck!* Try to be the best *you* that you can be, and you *will* be successful.

Affirmation #6

*I will discover ways
to accomplish my goals by learning
from others' mistakes.*

Getting Unstuck

Making It Personal to You

1. Take a look back over your life. List one to three choices
    you made that, had you known then what you know now,
    you would have made a different decision. Try to choose
    situations that you could have avoided by learning from
    other people's mistakes (whether you know the person
    personally or not).

    a. _____

    b. _____

    c. _____

2. Select one of the situations above. What could you have
    done differently to end up with a healthier, more positive
    outcome?_____

    _____

    _____

3. What can you or have you learned from this situation that
    you can teach others?_____

    _____

    _____

"Learn from the mistakes of others-you can never live long enough to make them all yourself."

John Luther

Knugget #7

Be honest with yourself.

Remember the old saying, "honesty is the best policy?" Well, that also includes being honest with yourself. Synonyms of the word honesty are frankness, openness, sincerity, integrity, responsibility and uprightness.

In order to get unstuck, one must be open and honest with oneself. Do you have a problem that you need to overcome but can't seem to control? You need to be open and honest with yourself and with God.

Oftentimes we do a very good job of excusing our weaknesses or negative characteristics. We find excuses as to why we made a negative statement or did something wrong. We justify instead of rectify. One of the first steps in correction is exposing the problem.

First, stand in front of the mirror and admit to yourself and God what your problem is. Don't be afraid. You are not less of a person but more of a person for facing the problem. *Second*, pray and ask God for help. You can't do this alone. *Third*, confide in someone. Someone you can trust who will hold you accountable (without holding it over your head), but keep your confidence.. *Fourth*, get rid of any items, or disassociate yourself from people that will pull you into the bottomless pit of guilt and despair.

Get unstuck! Try these four steps over and over again, until you are comfortable being honest with yourself.

Affirmation # 7

*I will tell myself the truth
because the truth will set me free.*

Getting Unstuck

Making It Personal to You

Be authentic (honest and open) while answering these questions. Share the real you.

1. Write down one thing about yourself that you have been hiding from others._____

   _____

2. Write down one thing about yourself that you would like to improve._____

   _____

3. Now write down one thing that you don't like about yourself._____

   _____

4. Are #1 and #3 the same thing?_____

5. Write down one thing about yourself that you are in denial about (*in other words, you don't like to admit to yourself or others that you do this or are like this*)?_____

   _____

6. Why are you hiding this part of you?_____

   _____

7. If you are unable to answer question #6, think about these simple questions.
   a. Is pride making you hide this part of you? _____
   b. Are you afraid that people won't like you?_____
   c. Have you been trying to live up to someone else's standard? _____
   d. Is there someone close to you that criticizes you? ___

   _____

8. Go back to question #6 and try to answer it again. Now go in front of a mirror and watch yourself as you say the following statement.

> *I am _____ (name the weakness), but I am still loveable. I will overcome this weakness over time, and I have taken the first step in being honest with myself.*

9. I don't want you to start focusing on the weakness. We should focus on building our strengths while managing our weaknesses. So let's end by focusing on one strength. What do you like about yourself?_____

10. If you can't answer question #9, then you need to ask your friends what they like about you. Everyone has strengths. Write down what your friends said. _____

_____

Once your friends tell you what they like, start to look in the mirror and tell yourself that you are this person. *Remember, God made us fearfully and wonderfully.*

Being authentic and honest with yourself means telling yourself the truth about your weaknesses and the truth about the parts of you that are loveable *(we are not talking about being conceited or narcissistic, but authentic, open, humble and honest with yourself).*

Doesn't that feel good inside? Don't be afraid. If it doesn't feel good, then over time it will. Now that you have been honest with yourself, work through whatever you need to work through to manage this weakness.

This is probably one of the hardest things you'll have to do in this book. Being authentic is hard for most of us, but it gets easier. I would encourage you to go through this chapter a few times.

11. Write a journal entry that expresses how you feel about looking at yourself in the mirror and being open and honest about whom you are.

Your Journal Entry

_____

_____

_____

_____

_____

_____

_____

Draw A Picture

Draw a picture below representing who you are striving to be (you don't have to be an artist). It can be a person, a scene, symbols, etc.

Knugget #8

Discover your *purpose.*

Know your *gifts.*

Y ou go to work, perform your duties, then come home. Despite spending the evening relaxing with family or even volunteering at a non-profit, the next day you go to work again... *unfulfilled*. You go home, and the pattern repeats itself. Too many people are in jobs feeling unfulfilled. Many have developed a routine that they perform on autopilot. I have a few important questions for you. What is your purpose or mission in life? What gifts and talents do you possess that are untapped?

God created each of us for a purpose. Your economic background, your ethnicity, size or shape doesn't play a role in this matter. We were each created with gifts and talents for a purpose. Do you know your purpose? Are your gifts and talents being utilized? You may ask yourself the question, *"how do I know what my purpose is in life?"* Or, *"what are my gifts?"* Start by asking yourself the questions in the **Getting Unstuck** section at the end of this Knugget. When you have asked and answered these questions, you will be on the road to discovering your purpose.

Once you are on the path to discovery, be courageous. *Get unstuck!* Don't be afraid to do something radical to achieve your goals. When all else fails, remember that God created you for a purpose. He has the ultimate plan, so ask Him for wisdom and guidance, then start moving forward. It will come to you step by step.

Affirmation # 8

I will discover my purpose
and live it fully.

Getting Unstuck

Making It Personal to You

1. If you were told you were going to receive one million dollars each year for the rest of your life, what would you do with that money (i.e. start a youth center)? _____

2. What games did you play as a child?_____

3. Was there anything you used to do that got you in trouble as a child (i.e. talk a lot)?_____

4. List something people tell you that you are good at doing or that comes naturally to you?_____

5. If you could conquer fear, what profession would you pursue?_____

6. What are you passionate about?_____

7. What do you enjoy doing in your free time?_____
_____

8. What activities do you enjoy doing?_____

9. What do you do for friends or family that others get paid for but you don't because you enjoy it?_____

10. If your circumstances were different (personal, financial, professional or spiritual) what profession would you be in right now?_____

11. What do people tell you, you should be doing?_____

12. What activity or profession excites you or makes your spirit jump when you watch or listen to someone else do it?_____

13. What talents or skills do you know you have?_____

14. What do you desire to do?_____

Take a look at your answers. Is there anything that keeps repeating itself. This could be something you should look into further. *Pursue your passion and you'll find your purpose.*

Knugget #9

Invest time, money and *wisdom* in yourself.

Y ou are priceless. Whether or not you know or believe it, you possess the ability to do great things within the purpose that God has set for your life. It doesn't matter what your circumstances are now, what others are saying or what you currently believe. You are a person of greatness. That said, you should spend time, money and wisdom on yourself. You are more than worth it.

Become a *personal growth investor*. Set goals, write out a plan, and then invest whatever time, wisdom, willpower and money is needed to achieve that goal. The rewards will be priceless. By the way, I'm not telling you to be selfish with your money. Not at all. I encourage giving to others. But what I am encouraging you to do is to also invest your money in helping *you* get unstuck (i.e motivational CD's, books, classes,etc.). If no one has ever told you that you are worth it, I'm telling you now. Repeat these affirmations to start you on the path of right thinking.

1. *I am fearfully and wonderfully made.*
2. *I was created for a purpose.*
3. *I will succeed.*

Start this process by investing time in yourself. Spend just a few minutes per day repeating these three affirmations. Begin investing in the wisdom that these statements possess. As mentioned in **Knugget #3**, to overcome insecurities, negative thinking and purposeless living, we must start with our thoughts first. You'll be more willing to invest the time, wisdom and money you need to *get unstuck* and reach your next level in life. Begin today by becoming a personal growth investor.

Affirmation #9

*I am valuable
and worth my investment.
I am fearfully and wonderfully made.*

Getting Unstuck

Making It Personal to You

1. Do you know what your purpose is?_____
   *If you answered "no" to question #1, go back to **Knugget #8** and review the questions in the **Getting Unstuck** section.*

2. Have you written out a plan to live your purpose?_____

3. If you answered "yes," do you know how much it will cost you at each step of the way to achieve your purpose / goal?_____

4. How much? Write it down._____

5. How much time do you plan to invest each day or each week to work toward achieving your purpose in life?____

   _____

6. What are you reading (or what do you plan to read) that relates to your purpose?_____

   _____

7. Are you going to pursue your purpose until you can make comfortable income?_____

8. Are you going to just pursue it as a hobby?_____

9. What other things can you do to invest time, money and wisdom into yourself and purpose?_____

   _____

   _____

Invest time, money and wisdom in yourself.
You are worth it!

Knugget #10

Help someone else, and one day *someone* else will help *you*.

Selfishness doesn't bring happiness. It leaves you uptight and without peace. We have to be accountable to someone or some system. Society thrives on interrelations. We each need assistance in one way or another, whether we are aware of it or not. That car you bought, did you pay by cash or do you have a loan? If you received a loan, someone had to approve your loan. That job that you possess, you had to interview or apply for it, right? You didn't just walk in off the street and start working. The air that you breathe, who is providing it? Helping others is one way to say thank you to those who have helped you in the past. It also provides a way to invest in yourself through helping someone else.

The other day I was standing in line at the Wal-Mart Business Center in my town, waiting to make copies. There were two people ahead of me. The clerk was very slow, and the time I had to get to my next meeting was quickly running out. I kindly informed the lady in front of me, *"I'm going to be late for a meeting, and I need to make some copies. Could I go ahead of you?"* "Sure," she answered. Then she chuckled and said, *"no one ever does that for me."* *"I'm sure someone will,"* I replied. She looked skeptical. I then shared that a few months ago, someone was in desperate need of getting out of the store, and I happily allowed her to go ahead of me in line. Now, months later, I'm reaping the rewards of helping someone else.

Don't look for your rewards, but understand that your reward for helping others will come when you need it most. Also, it may not come directly to you, but possibly to a family member. In fact, don't *look* for the rewards. My father is a good example of this. He has always had a heart for helping others. It's rooted deep in his soul. For him, it's almost as natural as breathing. However, when he helps others, he doesn't expect or want anything in return. My point is that we shouldn't help others and then expect something in return. Do it out of the goodness of your heart. *Get unstuck!* Help someone who needs help. It's one way to help you feel good deep down in your soul.

Affirmation #10

I will serve humankind.

Getting Unstuck

Making It Personal to You

1. Think about a time when someone helped you. Write down the situation._____

   _____

2. How did you feel when that person(s) helped you? _____

   _____

3. Write down one person or organization that you have been meaning to help but haven't gotten around to it.____

   _____

4. Now write down when you are going to help them. *If you don't plan it, in other words, carve out some time for it, it probably won't happen.*

   _____

   Now write the date down on a visible calendar or planner and tell a friend who will hold you accountable.

5. What are you going to do for this person or organization?

   _____

6. How much will it cost you?_____
7. How much time will you have to spend?_____
8. What will you get out of serving this person or helping this organization (*i.e. a sense of fulfillment, peace, joy, etc.?*)_

   _____

   _____

Here are a few things you can do to help others:
1. Find a non-profit organization and volunteer your services. It helps them and helps you to sharpen your skills.
2. Find creative ways to support your church, if you attend one.
3. Call an elderly neighbor. Find out if you can help them.

Knugget #11

Be a leader, not a follower.

Albert Einstein, Martin Luther King, Jr., Mother Teresa, Fidel Castro, Oprah Winfrey, the Wright Brothers, Rudolph Giuliani, Winston Churchill, Jackie Robinson, Adolf Hitler, Abraham Lincoln, Rosa Parks, Moses and Jesus. What do each of these individuals have in common? They are all recognized as leaders. They are or were leaders whose guidance influenced their community and the world, both in positive and negative ways.

These individuals have something else in common. They knew their purpose, and were not afraid to live for it. They weren't afraid to stand apart from the crowd, not in order to be a spectacle, but so that their personal mission, their purpose in life, could be fulfilled. They were willing to stand for what they believed in, and in doing so, they changed the course of history and will affect people's lives for years to come. Whether or not we agree with their political views or decisions, they are still leaders.

Some say a leader is created. Others say a leader is developed. I say if you live your purpose and know your personal mission in life, you will automatically be thrown into roles of leadership.

When we follow the masses, laws remain the same, societies become stagnant and progression is hindered. Anyone can be a follower. Be a leader in your corner. Stand for what is right. Live the purpose that you were created to live, and you will lead the people in your corner that you were destined to lead. I might add be a positive leader. A leader who will influence citizens to form a better society.

To be an effective leader, there are some key characteristics that you should posses. Review the list below and see how many describe you.

1. **Be a servant**. Help others.
2. **Be willing to listen to wisdom.** It can help you to avoid problems in the future.

3. **Be a life trainee**. Listen to the lessons that life is teaching you.

4. **Be an effective communicator.** It's not what you say, but how you say it. Be aware of your body language.

5. **Be willing to surround yourself with talented people.** Develop a team. We can't do it alone.

6. **Be comfortable with isolation or with standing alone.** It's in the quiet times that you grow the most.

7. **Be able to think out of the box**. That's what leaders do. They are not afraid to do the right things differently.

Affirmation #11

I will lead others
by living my purpose.

Getting Unstuck

Making It Personal to You

Leadership sometimes means standing alone (even when you make the right decision). Think about that as you answer the following questions.

1. Think of one decision that you made recently (or in your lifetime) that you didn't agree with but, not wanting to be the odd man out, agreed to. What should your decision have been?_____
   _____

2. How would this new decision have affected you back then?_____
   _____

3. Looking back, how does the decision you made then affect you now?_____
   _____
   _____

4. Was the decision you made then (even though you didn't agree with it) the right or wrong decision?
   _____

5. If you knew then what you know now, would you have stood alone?_____
   _____

6. If you knew then what you know now, would you have still followed the crowd, or would you have made another decision, even if you were standing alone?_____

Review what you have just written. Now think about how you can use the information to help you in the future.

"You don't have to hold a position in order to be a leader."

Anthony J. D'Angelo

Founder of the Collegiate Empowerment Company

Knugget #12

Stop making the same mistakes *everyone* around you is making. You already *know* the results.

Turn on the news and you will come across dozens of stories of people making the same mistake and getting the same results. Why do we insist on making the same mistakes that others have already made? Think back, have you ever knowingly made the same decision as someone else expecting a different outcome, only to find out later it was really the same mistake that garnered the same results? Isn't it funny how that works?!

Life is too short to experience everything. We need to get into the habit of using wisdom to solve our problems. As mentioned in previous Knuggets, use self-control and a little wisdom mixed with patience, and you will keep yourself out of many problems.

When you are in that split-second, decision-making moment, choose to look forward and think of what the consequences could be if you make the same mistake as someone else. *Choose long-term wisdom, peace and joy.* Although the price you pay may be tears, frustration or emotional pain, the heartache will pass. When the storm clouds clear, you will see that the sun was waiting to emerge.

Forward thinking, thinking about the future consequences of our choices, can save you from making a mistake that could last a lifetime. The life of your family, friends and even society can be altered forever from a bad decision. *Get unstuck!* Don't make the same mistake as others around you. You'll probably end up with the same results.

Affirmation #12

*I will learn from others' mistakes and
live beyond my mistakes.*

Getting Unstuck

Making It Personal to You

1. Write down one mistake that you keep making over and over again._____

2. Why do you continually make this mistake?_____
   _____

3. What will happen if you don't make this mistake? *I will...*
   _____
   _____

4. Does what you wrote in #3 resonate with your soul?_____

5. If yes, why does it ?_____

6. If no, why not?_____

7. Write down what actions you must take in order to avoid making the same mistake you made in #1 again._____
   _____

8. When are you going to start rectifying this mistake?_____
   _____

9. Who will help you?_____

You can do this. Dig down deep and find the determination in your heart to do the right thing.

Knugget #13

Don't choose the right *path* then go in the *wrong* direction.

Y ou're taking a road trip. You know where you need to end up. You have directions. You come to a crossroad. You turn left onto the correct street, only to find out 5 miles later that you are heading in the wrong direction. You should have turned right. When some of us come to the crossroads in our life, we end up on the right road to our destination, yet head in the wrong direction.

You may have determined your purpose but are diligently working away from it because you have surrounded yourself with the wrong people. People whom, with bad habits and bad advise, are not encouraging you but discouraging you. You may be on the right path but doing things the wrong way. Moving forward without the right training, the right products or the right equipment.

When you discover your purpose and know who you are created to be, begin your journey by reading as much as possible about how to proceed, what tools you need, the type of people that you need to support you, how much it will cost, etc. There are people out there who have taken similar roads to the one you are on. Discover who they are. Read their books. Attend their classes. Have lunch with them. Glean as much as you can from them. They will be able to help you avoid the mistakes that many have made and help ensure that you are pointed in the right direction.

Affirmation #13

*I will learn all there is to learn about
the direction that
I need to go.*

Getting Unstuck

Making It Personal to You

1. Make a list of magazines or books that will support your purpose/mission.

   _____

   _____

   _____

2. Perform an Internet search to find out any associations or e-zine subscriptions that you can join.   Now list them below:

   _____

   _____

   _____

3. Write down a training program or class that you need to take to help you head in the right direction._____

   _____

4. Who can you *shadow* or have lunch with to help you move in the right direction?_____

If you haven't already, consider signing up for one of my four empowering e-newsletters *(they're fre*e) to help you pattern your thoughts and plan your steps in the right direction. Visit **www.DivineDiscipline.com** .

Knugget #14

Where you are *going* has nothing to do with where you have been.

Some of us can say that we had a tough childhood. Many of us are living beyond our means through loans or credit cards. Some of us have people or situations in our family history that we don't necessarily feel happy revealing. Whatever your past situation, you don't have to allow it to shape your life. We hear stories everyday of people who overcame all odds. Each story is unique; the only common denominator is that the person got unstuck, reached beyond their limits, and found his or her purpose. These stories tell of people who made a conscious decision to not allow their past to dictate their future.

Your willpower can take you from poverty to riches; sickness to health; job to purpose. It may take years, blood, sweat and tears, but with determination you can be the first to go to college in your family, the first to purchase a car, the first to move out of the small dead-end town where you grew up. W. Clemont Stone said that a *"positive attitude is the big difference between success and failure."* Unfortunately, society causes many of us to subconsciously believe that everything can and should come quick and easily. Don't be fooled. The best things in life take time and effort. You don't have to allow your past mistakes or those of your family to dictate your destiny. Yes, it will be hard, but you can overcome anything you put your mind to. Decide today that you are not going to allow life to control you; you are going to take control of your life. Begin by reading books about the people who have reached the place you want to be.

Disassociate yourself from people who discourage you from following your dreams. Try to surround yourself with people who are on their way or are where you want to end up. Change your thinking so it aligns with your purpose. Write affirmations and positive confessions to start propelling your heart, mind and will in that direction. Don't allow your history to dictate your future. *Get unstuck* from your past. Let your new attitude, willpower and Divine guidance propel you to the fulfilling future that you deserve.

Affirmation #14

My past does not dictate my future.

Getting Unstuck

Making It Personal to You

We all have weaknesses or skeletons in our closet. Following these instructions will help you heal from past wounds.

1. Write down one thing from your past that is haunting you or that you are afraid to share with others *(if you are afraid to write it down for fear someone will find this book, say it out loud).*_____

   _____

2. Write down what you believe will happen the moment that people find out._____

   _____

3. Now write down how you think your interactions will go with people 3, 6 and 12 months after you have shared your secret._____

   _____

   _____

   _____

4. Would this *secret* stop you from pursuing your dreams, or would it just make life harder?_____

   _____

5. For most of us, our past choices may make it harder for us to pursue our goals, but can't stop us in our tracks. If your past were discovered, which of these character traits would make it harder?

   a. ____ my pride
   b. ____ my fear
   c. ____ my laziness
   d. ____ my selfishness
   e. ____ my doubt or disbelief
   f. ____ other reasons. Explain_____

You are destined for great accomplishments. Don't allow your pride, fear, laziness or selfishness to stop you. No one can stop you but you. People and situations can make things harder, but they can't stop you.

"Your past does not determine your future. It serves as a benchmark for what was and a lesson for where you are going"

Clestine I. Herbert

Knugget #15

Laziness will abort your

success or *eventually* kill you.

I n this country we have fast food, instant food, remote controls, the internet, cell phones and more. These items were apparently all designed to make life easier. However, now we have a generation that wants satisfaction immediately without working to get it. Now we expect things instantly. There are people whose laziness or impatience causes them to feel that if they have to work or wait for anything then they don't want it after all. Too many people are only interested in the quickest and easiest way to get to where they want to go. If something requires work and effort, they give up. When faced with a challenge, they think, *"is there a way this can be done without me having to do anything?"* Granted, these are broad statements; however, for many the principle is true. There is a proverb in the Bible that says, *"If you are too lazy to plow, don't expect a harvest."*[1]

Laziness not only zaps your energy, it brings poverty, crime and destruction. Laziness affects your health. Laziness programs your mind to lean toward negative thinking and plays the blame game. *Blaming others for your mishaps will never help you.* Instead, you must determine that you can and will overcome adversity through prayer, hard work and determination. Laziness procrastinates. Laziness tells you to sit down instead of get up. Laziness says, *"I can't,"* instead of, *"I can and I will."* Never abort hard work, abort laziness, and stay in the pursuit.

When you feel *drained or* the *lazy bug* bites you, try some of these techniques to build your energy and bite back:
1. Remind yourself that it won't get done unless you do it.
2. Generate some of your own energy by doing something you enjoy.
3. Play some music, then get up and sing or dance.
4. Get a friend to be your accountability partner to give you a gentle nudge now and then.
5. Go for a walk, then come back and start again.
6. Exercise your body and your mind.

---

[1] *Proverbs chapter 20 verse 4 of the Contemporary English Version Bible*

7. If you need to submit a proposal to someone, schedule a meeting with him or her and work toward that date.

8. Do something that is out of your normal routine. Oftentimes, it's the routine itself that will wear you out.

9. Write down the top three things you need to do today, then do them.

10. Don't think about how long it will take or how hard it might be. Just go into autopilot mode and do what is on your list.

11. Ask yourself why you are feeling lazy. Is it a physical or emotional problem?

12. Call a friend whose energy will help to energize you.

13. Read an inspiring book.

14. Listen to inspiring or upbeat, positive music.

15. Listen to a motivational or spiritually uplifting CD.

16. Eat a healthy meal (i.e. salad)

17. Drink lots of water.

Get unstuck by aborting laziness
and increasing your energy.

Affirmation #15

I will work toward achieving my long-term goals by accomplishing my daily tasks.

Getting Unstuck

Making It Personal to You

Let's analyze why you are feeling lazy or why your energy is drained. Be open and honest with yourself. The process works better that way.

1. Are you generally a sluggish person?_____

2. Does your laziness occur after you eat? _____

3. How about after a discouraging moment?_____

4. After a late night?_____

5. What happens in that moment of laziness *(what are you feeling, what are you saying to yourself, etc.)*?_____

    _____

    _____

This is just a start to get you thinking about what could be triggering your laziness or energy drain. Use the space below to record more about why you feel this way.

"The soul of a lazy man desires, and has nothing; But the soul of the diligent shall be made rich."

A Biblical Proverb

Proverbs 13:4 New King James Version

Knugget #16

Get used to doing *positive* things that *you* don't like doing.

While you are on the road to your purpose and success, you will discover that wisdom will, in the long run, save you much pain. You may have to make sacrifices now to reap rewards later. You will probably have to do a lot of reading, but the wisdom you gain will be priceless. You may have to limit your social life, but when compared to the incomparable reward of accomplishing your goal, it's a small sacrifice. Eating healthy and exercising will provide the energy and stamina you need to succeed.

Get used to doing positive things that provide positive, lasting results. It may be painful at first but, just like any other habit, eventually it will become routine. Once you get used to it, any discomfort will dissipate, and you will become a better person for it.

Throughout this book, I have offered you the cognitive tools and successful behaviors needed to live a fulfilling, successful life. You may not want to do some of the things that I have shared. You may *feel* like you don't want to do them. You may *feel* like you don't have the energy to do them. However, in order to get unstuck, you must not always let your feelings guide you. It is more about doing what is right. You may start out by not wanting to do what is right, but eventually, with repetition and perseverance, it will become a habit, and hopefully something you enjoy. You can *choose* to stay stuck or you can *choose* to get unstuck and start living that fulfilling successful life that you were designed to live. It is *your* choice.

Affirmation #16

*I will do what is best for me
spiritually, personally & professionally so
that I can live the fulfilling life
I was created to live.*

Getting Unstuck

Making It Personal to You

1. What good habit are you going to spend the next three months developing (pick just one)?_____

   _____

2. How do you plan to develop this habit? List the steps that you will take:
   a. Step 1:_____
   b. Step 2:_____
   c. Step 3:_____

3. What negative habit are you going to spend the next three months eliminating or overcoming?_____

   _____

4. Write down the steps you will take to overcome this negative habit:

   a. Step 1:_____
   b. Step 2:_____
   c. Step 3: _____

5. Who will you solicit to help you or hold you accountable for overcoming this habit?_____

   _____

6. What or who will motivate you to help you continue to break the negative habit while fostering a positive one?

   _____

   _____

Align yourself with the positive things that will propel you forward to the successful life you were designed for.

A Final Message To You

Getting Unstuck

This little book was written to jumpstart you into *getting unstuck.* It is meant to serve as a way for learning how to use cognitive tools and develop successful attitudes and behaviors. It was designed to be an appetizer for your journey to success. I hope it has created a spark that will inspire you to discover more about you, your potential, your passion and your purpose.

While reading this book you have hopefully discovered more about who you are now and who you are destined to become. Don't stop here. Continue to learn and grow. And don't forget to enjoy the journey.

I hope that we will meet again through one of my future books, CDs or DVDs. Or perhaps we will meet during one of my coaching programs, teleclasses, seminars or keynote addresses. Whatever the case may be, I hope this is the beginning of an empowering relationship.

Empowerment is something that should be shared. Share what you discovered with a friend, family member or colleague. Better yet, share what you have discovered with me. I love to hear how people are discovering, learning and growing. Visit my website at www.DivineDiscipline.com or contact me at Clestine@DivineDiscipline.com to tell me about your journey.

If you would like a visual display of the *16 Knuggets* shared in this book as a daily reminder to empower you, invest in the **Knuggets of Knowledge Poster**. This full-color poster makes a great gift to yourself or someone you love and is available for purchase on our product page at www.DivineDiscipline.com. I look forward to our next encounter together. Until then, stay F.E.D.... *Focused, Empowered, Determined!*

*Clestine, The Purpose Coach
and Empowerment Speaker*

Epilogue

In God We Trust

I magine you're listening to the radio as you take a road trip. As you get out of range, the voices get fuzzy, and you can no longer hear the dialogue or music. All you can hear is static. This is similar to how many of us are currently relating to God. Some of us are *out of range* and wondering why we are unable to hear the voice of God. We're wondering why we don't know which direction to turn or which path to pursue. Others are not really concerned about whether or not God's voice can be heard clearly. They have already switched to another channel for clearer reception. In other words, some people seek out other ways to try to experience love, power, prosperity, and peace. However, in the long run, these alternate sources can bring defeat, tragedy, or pain.

The deaths that occurred following 9/11, the Indian Ocean tsunami, Hurricane Katrina, and the collapse of the West Virginia mines were tragic and brought nations to their knees. The entire world was affected, and survivors were left devastated and confused, calling out God's name. On National TV, politicians sang songs to God while praying to *"the One we trust."* These tragedies brought people to churches in flocks, all praying for His intervention, His comfort, His wisdom, strength and safety.

American currency touts, **"In God We Trust."** But do we? There's no doubt we run to Him after a tragedy, but do we trust that He created us and knows the direction we should be going? Do we trust that He will guide us in the right direction? Do we really trust Him? Our currency seems to indicate that we do. But some of our actions would indicate otherwise.

If we feel we can call on Him during these hard times, don't you think it would be good to call on Him for guidance, strength, wisdom and assistance *before* and during the journey to your purpose? Why wait until problems arise, such as getting stuck or while facing a tragedy? Ask Him for help before trouble begins and you will see His guidance toward your purpose. Ask Him for help now. It is as simple as saying, *"Lord, please help me."* Now request His help so you can start enjoying His love and guidance while you enjoy your journey. His love is always there and His guidance is always available.

Affirmations To Get Unstuck

Continuing the Journey

N ow that you have read this book, let me continue to help you to remain on the path to success. Read these affirmations each morning and each evening. Say them during the day when you need an extra boost. Share them with friends that need encouragement. Get unstuck and *reach beyond your limits* to the next level of your success. And remember to enjoy the journey!

Affirmation#1: *I will take my knowledge and turn it into power by taking calculated risks.*

Affirmation#2: *I will maintain the knowledge I have acquired by using it repeatedly and sharing it with others.*

Affirmation#3: *I will take control of my thoughts before my thoughts take control of me.*

Affirmation#4: *I will own my behavior.*

Affirmation#5: *I choose wisdom over my feelings.*

Affirmation#6: *I will discover ways to accomplish my goals by learning from others' mistakes.*

Affirmation#7: *I will tell myself the truth because the truth will set me free.*

Affirmation#8: *I will discover my purpose and live it fully.*

Affirmation#9: *I am valuable and worth my investment. I am fearfully and wonderfully made.*

Affirmation#10: *I will serve humankind.*

Affirmation#11: *I will lead others by living my purpose.*

Affirmation#12: *I will learn from others' mistakes and live beyond my mistakes.*

Affirmation#13: *I will learn all there is to learn about the direction that I need to go.*

Affirmation#14: *My past does not dictate my future.*

Affirmation#15: *I will work toward achieving my long-term goals by accomplishing my daily tasks.*

Affirmation#16: *I will do what is best for me spiritually, personally and professionally so that I can live the fulfilling life I was created to live.*

If you enjoy saying these affirmations out loud, then you'll also enjoy the **Knuggets of Knowledge poster**. This poster has all sixteen (16) knuggets *(the chapter titles of this book)* displayed in a bright, full-color poster. It's a great way to help empower you each day.

Want More Ways to
Help You Get Unstuck?

If you enjoyed this book, consider these other programs and products to help you develop success attitudes and behaviors in any area of life:

The Official Programs of

- **Four FREE e-newsletters** – Choose from one or more of our mailing lists to receive the empowerment that you need.
    - *Thought of the Week*: weekly e-quote from Clestine
    - *Reach Beyond*: personal & professional development weekly e-newsletter with articles, featured products and events
    - *The D-Line*: quarterly professional development e-newsletter with empowering articles
    - *The Aroma of Christ*: monthly e-newsletter with spiritual and practical food for your soul

- **The Empowerment Club** – Each month discover positive attitude and success tools to help you succeed in any area of life. Hear from *Clestine, The Purpose Coach* & guest experts, as well as receive special offers, exclusive products at this empowering monthly tele-program (*over the phone*).

- **The 21-Day Challenge** – This is a fast-paced, four-week tele-coaching program *(four consecutive Tuesday evenings over the phone)* designed to help build momentum and motivation to achieve a small goal or create a habit.

- **Coaching Programs** – Get life coaching from *Clestine, the Purpose Coach.* Choose from four coaching plans to fit your schedule and budget.

- **Keynotes and Seminars** – Book Clestine to bring one of her highly interactive and engaging seminars or keynotes to your corporation, professional association meeting, college or church. Ask about our signature program *Reach Beyond Your Limits*™.

- **Reach Beyond Your Limits**™ program – This three-phase program consists of seminars, keynotes, CDs, books and more. Seminars and keynotes are as follows:
  o **Reach Beyond Your Limits**
  o **Think Beyond:** *The Power of Your Attitude*
  o **Plan Beyond:** *Designing a Goal Achievement Plan*
  o **Perform Beyond:** *Learning to Manage Your Energy*

- **Empowerment Products** – CDs, DVDs, workbooks, books, e-books and more.

To find out more about these programs,
*visit our website at **www.DivineDiscipline.com**,*
*email us at **Info@DivineDiscipline.com** or call **813-343-4112.***

Quick Order Form

Online orders: www.DivineDiscipline.com
Go to the product page.

Fax orders: Fax this form to: 1-866-525-1237.

Telephone orders: Call 1-813-343-4112.

Email orders: Info@DivineDiscipline.com

Postal Orders: Divine Discipline
P.O. Box 4019,
Spring Hill, Florida 34611, USA

I would like to order the following product(s). (*Please indicate the quantity*):

____   Knuggets of Knowledge to Get Unstuck, *$14.95*

____   Knuggets of Knowledge Poster, *$14.99*

____   Knuggets of Knowledge book and poster, *$24.99*
Please add $5.00 for shipping and handling in the U.S or Canada, or $10.00 for International Orders. Please call or email us regarding bulk orders.

Name:_____
Mailing Address:_____
City:_____ State: _____ Zip:_____
Telephone:_____
Email address*:_____

When you purchase our products, you will automatically be added to our **Thought of the Week mailing list, which features one empowering quote each Monday morning from Clestine, The Purpose Coach. **You will not be added to anyone else's mailing list.** We don't believe in SPAM, but know that the quotes will enhance your motivation throughout your success growth.*

Total Cost of your order:_____

Payment:

□ Check or □ Money Order

(Make all checks or money orders out to: Divine Discipline)

□ Credit Card: □Visa □Master Card □Discover

□American Express

Name as it appears on card:_____

Card Number: _____

Exp. Date: _____ Card Verf#:_____

Billing Address *(if different from the mailing address):*

_____

_____

How Else Can Clestine Help You Get Unstuck?:

We also provide seminars, tele-programs and coaching for professional, personal and spiritual development in the areas of:

- Leadership
- Success Attitudes and Behaviors
- Planning/Goal Achievement
- Positive Attitudes
- Performance Improvement/Energy/Motivation
- Employee Morale/Employee Motivation
- Employee Retention

Please *email* me more information on:

□ Keynote Speaking

□ Tele-programs *(over the phone)*

□ Seminars

□ Life Coaching

□ Achievement/Performance Development Consulting

Book Clestine, the Purpose Coach, to empower your church, corporation, professional association or community event.

Contact us at 813-343-4112 or Info@DivineDiscipline.com to order a book or to find out more.

More Empowering Products

To help you get unstuck

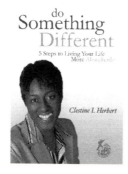

3245468

Made in the USA